With gratuitous gratitude to P.J.. whose clowning around was the aspiration for these patterns:
and to my family. which fuels my drive when the rubber hits the road.

Author: CJ McDonald
Designer: Deena Fleming

Copyright © 2006 Scholastic Inc.

Tangerine
Press
an imprint of
SCHOLASTIC
www.scholastic.com

Scholastic and Tangerine Press and associated logos are trademarks of Scholastic Inc
Published by Tangerine Press. an imprint of Scholastic Inc:
557 Broadway: New York. NY 10012

Scholastic Australia
Gosford NSW

10 9 8 7 6 5 4 3 2

ISBN 0-439-85344-3
Printed and bound in China

MAKE A PREHISTORIC AIR PET!

Ever wish you had lived in the days when prehistoric creatures roamed the earth – when Tyrannosaurus rex was the neighborhood bully, when Velociraptors were the neighborhood gang. when saber-toothed tigers were the neighborhood strays?

Okay, so maybe you could live without checking your datebook to see who's going to have you for lunch, but how about prehistoric pets that are all bubble and no bite? We'll show you how to let your imagination "saur" as you master the most terrible lizards and bring a woolly mammoth down to size.

Ready to put a twist on extinction? Let's get started on making you an official prehistoric park ranger!

CONTENTS

Difficulty Scale

Easy	Medium	Tricky

Fill 'Er Up

Your kit contains everything you need to start your own prehistoric zoo, including over 30 balloons, a balloon pump, and four sets of googly eyes to put the finishing touches on your dinosaurs! Besides all the goodies in your kit, you'll need some pipe cleaners, which you can pick up at your nearest craft store. Your predatory pets begin with a pump and long, skinny balloons called 260s. If you run out of balloons, don't sweat it. Just make a trip to your nearest party store.

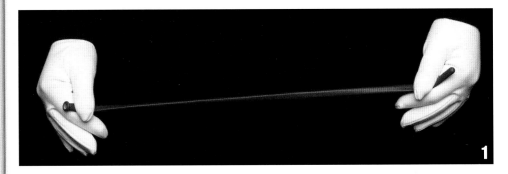

1) Before you pump your balloons, take a stretch. Grab a balloon by each end. The closed end is the tail, and the open end is the nozzle. Now, stretch the balloon across your chest. This gives it extra length and makes it, well, stretchier – both of which make it easier to work with.

2) Next, gently slide the nozzle over the tip of the pump. Holding the balloon onto the tip with your opposite hand, start pumping with the other hand. Keep pumping until you have a tiny stub (½ inch, or 1.25 cm) at the other end. The stub helps prevent a pop, which is never music to your ears. So let's be safety-savvy, and never fully inflate a balloon.

Holding the nozzle with one hand, carefully slide it off the pump with the other, pinching it together about 2 inches (5 cm) from the nozzle as it is released.

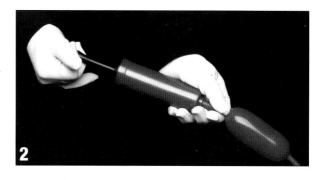

3) Let the air out to the point of the pinch, holding it tightly between your fingers. You've just burped your balloon! Now tie off the nozzle, and you're ready to learn some twisted logic!

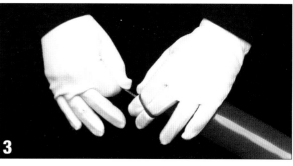

Twisted Logic

To be king over your dino domain, remember that practice rules. Don't make like a Pteranodon and just wing it. Start by pumping up a few 260s, some with tails and some with stubs. It's time to practice twisting.

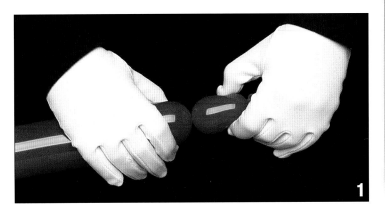

Most of the balloons in this book call for tails, the uninflated end of a balloon – sometimes a stub, sometimes several inches, depending on the pattern. Just leave uninflated whatever length tail is required, and tie off.

Bubble

1) This one is easy. To make a 1-inch (2.5-cm) bubble, hold your balloon in one hand.
2) Using your other hand, pinch your fingers down about 1 inch from the nozzle.
3) Then twist. You have a bubble. Remember that you must always twist in the same direction, or you'll undo your previous twists. And always hold the first and last bubbles in a series, or you'll experience that scientific principle about every action having an equal and opposite reaction.

Loop-twist

1) Here's a technique you'll use often to make armored plates, or even ears or legs. Hold your 1-inch (2.5-cm) bubble with one hand, and make a 4-inch (10-cm) bubble just beyond it. Remember always to hold your first and last bubbles – in this case, your first and second.

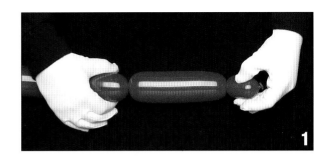

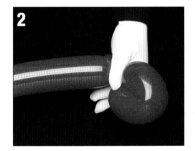

2) Fold the 4-inch (10-cm) bubble in half so the beginning twist and the last twist line up.

3) Twist the ends together at the joints to form a loop-twist. (Please note: In our patterns, the size of the loop-twist is the length of this original bubble, so we would call this a 4-inch (10-cm) loop-twist.)

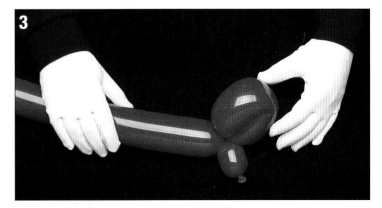

Some of the patterns call for specific dark colors, such as black. Trouble is, when balloons are uninflated, black, purple, green, and blue can all look alike. So here's a tip: Pump a tiny bit of air into the tail of a balloon to determine its color before starting your project.

Lock-twist

1) Make a 2-inch (5-cm) bubble and two 3-inch (7.5-cm) bubbles just beyond the loop twist. Fold the 3-inch bubbles down.

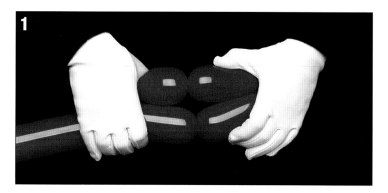

2) Twist the bubbles together at the joints. Doubled bubbles are no toil or trouble!

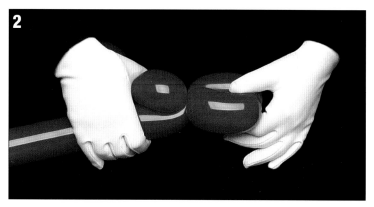

Tulip-twist

1) Get another 260 and hold the balloon with one hand. Using the other hand, push the nozzle into the balloon with your index finger. Pinch down on the nozzle with your first hand, and pull your index finger out of the nozzle.

2) Then make a 1-inch (2.5-cm) bubble. It's the case of the disappearing nozzle!

Curl

1) Here's how to bend the rules for shaping heads, necks, horns, or tails. Using the same or another 260, coil the balloon like a hose, starting at the nozzle-end. Squish it down a little to increase its turning curve.

2) Now release it. No curlers required!

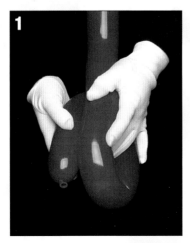

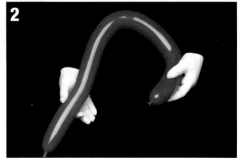

Soften

1) You should "soften" your balloons before every project. This gives the balloon more "give" when you're doing lots of twists, and it decreases the pop factor. Using a balloon with at least a 1-inch (2.5-cm) tail, gently squeeze the air from the middle of the balloon . . .

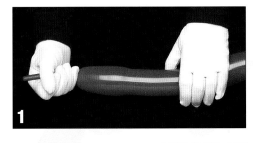

2) . . . to the end.

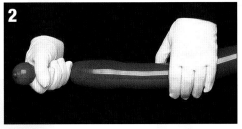

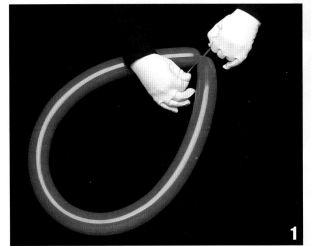

Circle-twist

1) Using the 260 you just softened, hold the tail in one hand and the nozzle in the other. Tie them together in a knot. You have the perfect shape for the base of wings or ears for larger air pets.

Twist

1) Holding the circle-twist in one hand, pinch your thumb and index finger together at the center of the balloon.

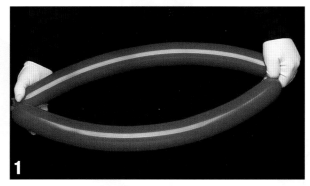 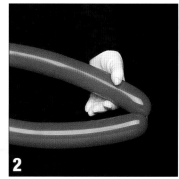

2) Twist at that point.

Ear-twist

This trick takes a little practice! It locks a bubble in place and also gives your creations a neater finish.

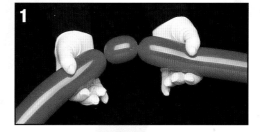

1) Make a 1-inch (2.5-cm) bubble in the middle of your circle-twist.

2) Then pinch it between your thumb and index finger—just like your aunt does to your cheek. Pull it up, and twist it around about five times to be sure it's secure.

A-PHAT-OSAUR

In a race for the highest, greenest leaves, the Apatasaurus will win by a neck!

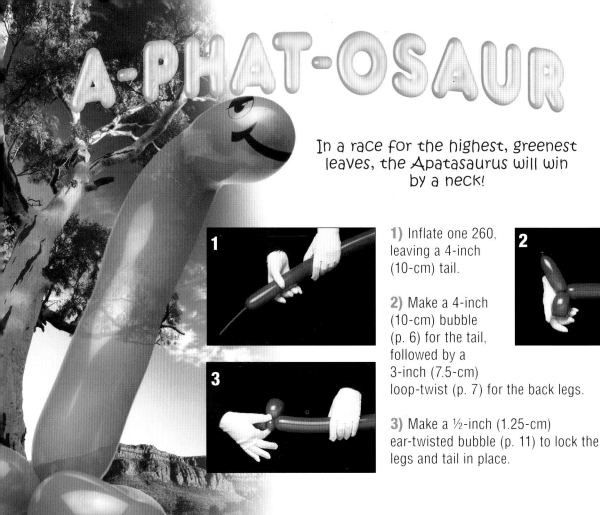

1) Inflate one 260, leaving a 4-inch (10-cm) tail.

2) Make a 4-inch (10-cm) bubble (p. 6) for the tail, followed by a 3-inch (7.5-cm) loop-twist (p. 7) for the back legs.

3) Make a ½-inch (1.25-cm) ear-twisted bubble (p. 11) to lock the legs and tail in place.

4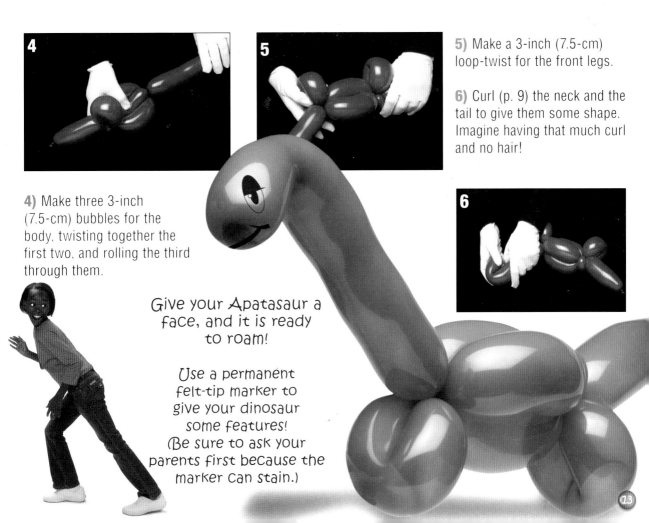

5

5) Make a 3-inch (7.5-cm) loop-twist for the front legs.

6) Curl (p. 9) the neck and the tail to give them some shape. Imagine having that much curl and no hair!

4) Make three 3-inch (7.5-cm) bubbles for the body, twisting together the first two, and rolling the third through them.

6

Give your Apatasaur a face, and it is ready to roam!

Use a permanent felt-tip marker to give your dinosaur some features! (Be sure to ask your parents first because the marker can stain.)

THEY CALL HIM FLIPPER

If you lived in the sea, watch out! You might have become the Plesiosaurus' prey.

1) Inflate three 260s, the first with a 3-inch (7.5-cm) tail and two more, of which you'll inflate only 10-inches (25-cm).

2) Make a 10-inch (25-cm) bubble (p. 6) at the nozzle-end of the first balloon for the neck.

3) Make two ½-inch (1.25-cm) ear-twisted bubbles (p. 11).

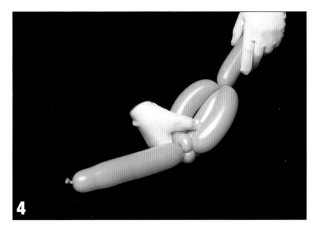

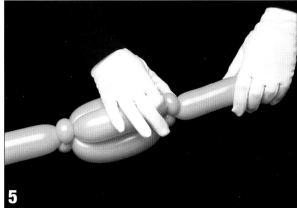

4) Make three 6-inch (15-cm) bubbles, twisting together the first two, and rolling the third through them.

5) To lock the body in place, make two ½-inch (1.25-cm) ear-twisted bubbles at the back of the body.

6) Using the 10-inch (25-cm) balloons, make two 5-inch (12.5-cm) bubbles in each, and let go. Yes, let go!

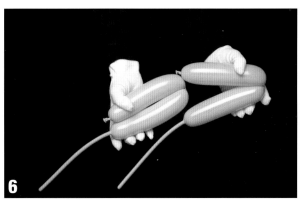

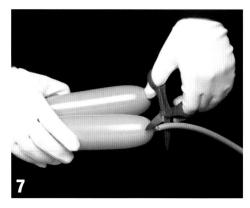

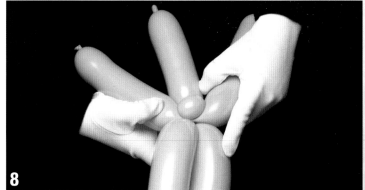

7) Tie a knot at the tail-end of each 10-inch (25-cm) balloon, and cut off the excess tail.

8) Your balloons have a little "give" where they were divided before. Divide one balloon in half again, and twist there. Wrap one around the joint between the body and neck of the first balloon.

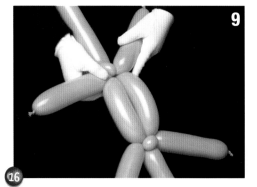

9) Divide the other balloon in half, and twist there. Wrap it around the tail joint. Now your Plesiosaur has flippers.

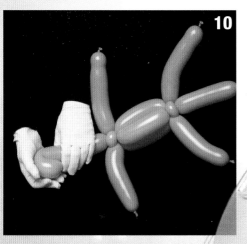

10

10) Curl (p. 9) the neck and add some eyes and a mouth. Look out!

Don't let this aquatic predator near your goldfish!

ANKYL BITER

Short and stout, the armored Ankylosaurus had a clubbed tail that meant anything but fun to its attackers!

1) Inflate four 260s, one with a 3-inch (7.5-cm) tail, the second of the same color with a 4-inch (10-cm) tail, and the third and fourth using a contrasting color with 6-inch (15-cm) tails.

2) Make a 3-inch (7.5-cm) bubble (p. 6) on the nozzle-end of the first balloon for a head.

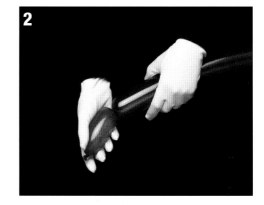

3) To begin the body, make two 6-inch (15-cm) bubbles, and twist them together.

4) Make one more 6-inch (15-cm) bubble, rolling it through the football-shaped body.

5) Then make one more 6-inch (15-cm) bubble, twisting it around the head joint to complete the body.

6

6) Using scissors, carefully cut off the remaining section of balloon. Tie it, and twist the uninflated section through the body and around the neck.

7

7) Using the second balloon, tie the nozzle-end around the neck joint of the first balloon.

8

8) Make a ¾-inch (1.9-cm) ear-twisted bubble (p. 11) to lock the neck in place.

9

9) Make a 1 ½-inch (3.75-cm) bubble and a ½-inch (1.25-cm) ear-twisted bubble near the neck to begin the series of spikes. Now repeat that bubble series twice more until spikes reach the tail.

10) Wrap the remaining section of the second balloon through the body.

11) Make a 4-inch (10-cm) bubble on what is now the tail.

12) Make two ½-inch (1.25-cm) bubbles and ear-twist them.

13) Using scissors, cut off the tail end of that balloon. Tie it, and cut off the excess.

14) It's time to make legs using one of the remaining balloons. Make two ½-inch (1.25-cm) bubbles, ear-twisting the second one and then the first one by twisting the nozzle around it.

15) Make a 1-inch (2.5-cm) bubble and a ¾-inch (1.9-cm) ear-twisted bubble.

16) Then make two 1 ½-inch (3.75-cm) bubbles and another ear-twisted ¾-inch (1.9-cm) bubble. Don't come undone when those bigger bubbles come undone. You'll be retwisting them in a minute.

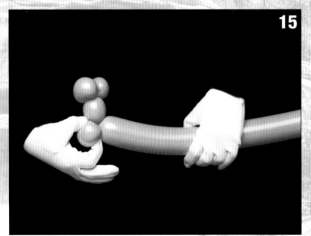

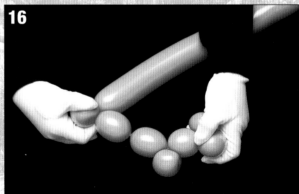

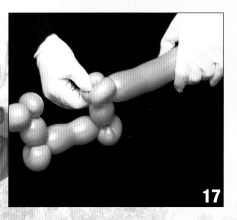

17) Make a 1-inch (2.5-cm) bubble and two more ear-twisted ½-inch (1.25-cm) bubbles. Your front legs are almost complete.

18) Using scissors, cut off the tail of that balloon. Tie a knot near the last ear-twist, and cut off the remaining end of the balloon.

19) Retwist those middle bubbles (notice the "give" the balloon now has there), and twist the legs one at a time beneath the neck joint of the first balloon.

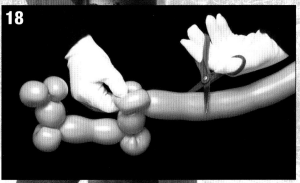

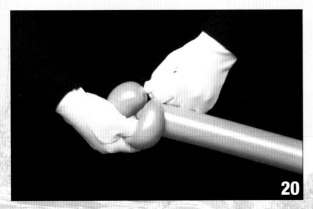

20) Having only one set of legs would be a drag for our dino, so let's give it a second set. Using the fourth balloon, make two ¾-inch (1.9-cm) bubbles, ear-twisting the second one, and then twist the nozzle around the first one.

21) Make a 1 ½-inch (3.75-cm) bubble and a ¾-inch (1.9-cm) bubble, ear-twisting the ¾-inch (1.9-cm) bubble.

22) Then make two 1 ½-inch (3.75-cm) bubbles and another ear-twisted ¾-inch (1.9-cm) bubble. Again, your middle bubbles will come undone.

23) Make a 1 ½-inch (3.75-cm) bubble and two more ear-twisted ¾-inch (1.9-cm) bubbles, and then cut off the excess with scissors.

24) Retwist the middle bubbles, and connect the second set of legs between them under the joint of the back of the body, adjusting as needed.

This re-invented reptile is ready to rumble!

The terrible Tyrannosaurus rex
isn't as fierce when you can't
see its teeth!

1) Inflate two 260s, leaving 4-inch (10-cm) tails.

2) Make a 3-inch (7.5-cm) bubble and a 4-inch (10-cm) bubble (p. 6) on the nozzle-end for the mouth.

3) Fold them together, and twist the nozzle around the joint to form jaws. Don't worry; your fingers are safe!

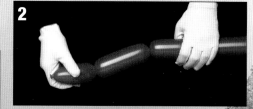

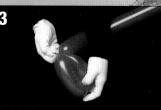

4) Make a 1-inch (2.5-cm) bubble, and ear-twist it (p. 11) behind the jaws for our lizard's tiny brain.

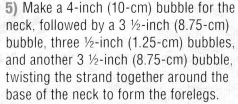

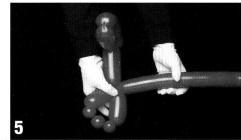

5) Make a 4-inch (10-cm) bubble for the neck, followed by a 3 ½-inch (8.75-cm) bubble, three ½-inch (1.25-cm) bubbles, and another 3 ½-inch (8.75-cm) bubble, twisting the strand together around the base of the neck to form the forelegs.

6) Ear-twist bubbles 2 and 4 (the outer ½-inch, or 1.25-cm, bubbles), and then divide the bubbles in half and ear-twist again.

7) Make a ½-inch (1.25-cm) bubble, and lock-twist it (p. 8) behind the base of the neck and the forelegs.

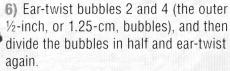

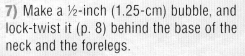

8) Using the second 260, make a 5-inch (12.5-cm) bubble, three ½-inch (1.25-cm) bubbles, and another 5-inch (12.5-cm) bubble on the nozzle-end to make the back legs. Tie the nozzle around the joint of the last bubble.

9) Repeat Step 6 (p. 27) to complete the back legs.

10) On the first balloon, make a 5-inch (12.5-cm) bubble just below the base of the neck and forelegs. Lock the back legs around at that twist. Next, make a ½-inch (1.25-cm) ear-twist to lock the legs in place.

11) Make another 5-inch (12.5-cm) bubble on the second balloon. Twist it at the neck. Then repeat that step, locking the last body bubble around the joint of the back legs.

12) Using scissors, cut off the remaining section of the second balloon, leaving a 2-inch (5-cm) piece of uninflated balloon. Tie it off and twist it through the body.

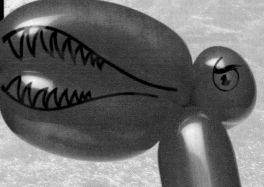

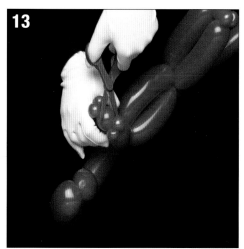

13

14

14) A fierce dinosaur needs a deep chest from which to roar. So adjust the bubbles of the body as needed.

13) Cut the middle bubble in the forelegs and back legs to separate and let our T. rex stand tall.

Don't forget to add some teeth. You've got this lizard down to a T!

PTERROR OF THE SKIES

The Pteranodon may no longer be in the air, but it doesn't have to be *out* of air!

1) Inflate two 260s, the first with a 4-inch (10-cm) tail and the second with a 1-inch (2.5-cm) tail.

2) Make a 4-inch (10-cm) bubble (p. 6) on the nozzle-end of the first balloon, bending it down to give it shape for a head.

3) Make two 5-inch (12.5-cm) bubbles, locking them together. Then make another 5-inch bubble, rolling it through the other bubbles to form the body.

4) Make a five-bubble series: one 2 ½-inch (6.25-cm) bubble, three ½-inch (1.25-cm) bubbles and another 2 ½-inch (6.25-cm) bubble, twisting the series onto the last bubble of the body.

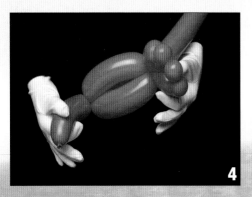

6) Using scissors, cut the middle bubble in the back legs.

5) Ear-twist (p. 11) the outer two ½-inch (1.25-cm) bubbles. Now that it has legs, it's time to take a stand!

7) Using the second 260, fold the inflated portion of the balloon in half and twist there.

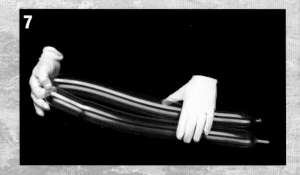

8

This bird is ready to fly! Help the Pteranodon catch its prey by giving it googly eyes.

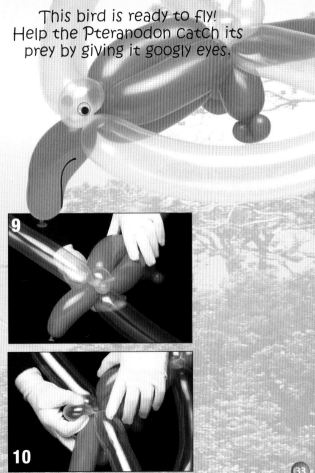

8) Make a 1-inch (2.5-cm) bubble in the middle and ear-twist it.

9) Squeeze the air to the end, leaving only a ¼-inch (.63-cm) tail. Lock that joint around the neck, leaving the 1-inch (2.5-cm) bubble at the top.

10) Make a ½-inch (1.25-cm) bubble and an 8-inch (20-cm) bubble on either end of the second balloon, and twist the joint of the smaller bubble around the joint of the back legs. Adjust the back legs and tail as needed.

SPIKEORSPEARUS

The Stegosaurus may look mean, but don't worry – this prehistoric pet prefers to eat plants!

1) Inflate two 260s. leaving a 4-inch (10-cm) tail on the first and a 5-inch (12.5-cm) tail on the second.

2) Make a 3-inch (7.5-cm) bubble (p. 6) on the nozzle-end of the balloon with the 4-inch (10-cm) tail for the head.

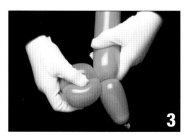

3) Make two 2 ½-inch (6.25-cm) bubbles for the legs. twisting them together.

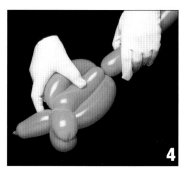

4) Begin the body with two 5-inch (12.5-cm) bubbles. locking them together. Then make a third 5-inch (12.5-cm) bubble. rolling it through to complete the body.

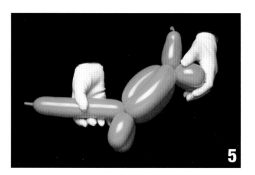

5) To make the back legs. make two 3 ½-inch (6.25-cm) bubbles. twisting them together.

6) Make two ½-inch (1.25-cm) ear-twisted bubbles (p. 11).

7) Using the second balloon, wrap the nozzle around the neck of your Stegosaurus.

7

8

8) Make a 1-inch (2.5-cm) bubble, followed by a ½-inch (1.25-cm) ear-twist. Repeat the series two more times, ending with a 1-inch (2.5-cm) bubble that you will twist around the last joint of the body.

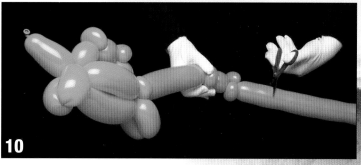

9) To make the clubbed tail, make a 6-inch (15-cm) bubble, two ½-inch (1.25-cm) ear-twisted bubbles, a 1 ½-inch (3.75-cm) bubble, and two more ear-twisted ½-inch (1.25-cm) bubbles.

10) Using scissors, cut off the remaining portion of the tail, twisting it around the ear-twists to hide it. Camouflage is important among plant-eaters!

11) Cut an uninflated balloon in half, and tie a knot on one end. Carefully insert a 5-inch (12.5-cm) section of pipe cleaner into each half of the balloon, and tie the other ends.

12) Twist the pipe cleaner sections around the ear-twist joints of the tail to create spikes.

Add some googly eyes to your Stegosaurus for the perfect plant predator!

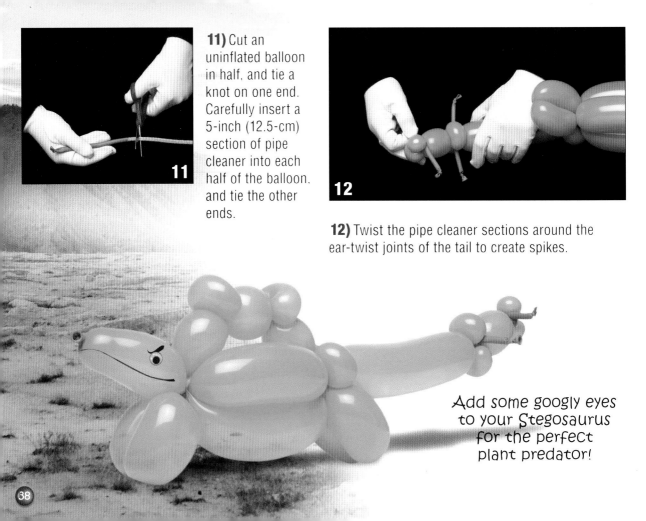

RUBBER RAPTOR

Don't be afraid of this Velociraptor. Rubber raptors rarely live up to the bad raps earned by their namesake!

1) Inflate two 260s, the first with a 4-inch (10-cm) tail and the second with a 6-inch (15-cm) tail.

2) Make a 2-inch (5-cm) bubble (p. 6) and a ½-inch (1.25-cm) ear-twist (p. 11) at the nozzle-end.

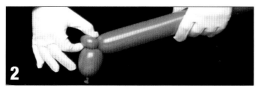

3) Now make a 4-inch (10-cm) bubble and a ¾-inch (1.875-cm) ear-twist.

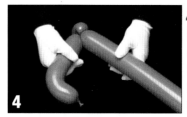

4) Carefully undo the ½-inch (1.25-cm) ear-twist (just twist in the opposite direction), and your 2-inch (10-cm) bubble comes undone. Now the head has some shape.

7) With the body complete, you're ready for legs. Using the second balloon, make a 1-inch (2.5-cm) bubble at the nozzle-end, wrapping the nozzle around the joint and tucking it in. You just ear-twisted your bubble. Then divide that bubble in half (stick your fingers deep into the middle gently but firmly) and make two ½-inch (1.25-cm) ear-twists with it.

5) Make three 5-inch (12.5-cm) bubbles, twisting the first two together and rolling the third one through the conjoined pair.

6) Make two ½-inch (1.25-cm) ear-twists at the base of the body. Position them on either side of the body to lock it in place.

8) Now get ready for the World Series of Bubbles! Make a 3-inch (7.5-cm) bubble, a ½-inch (1.25-cm) ear-twisted bubble, a 2-inch (5-cm) bubble, and another ½-inch (1.25-cm) ear-twisted bubble. Take a deep breath, because you're not **done yet!**

9) Make two ½-inch (1.25-cm) bubbles. (These will come undone, but it's okay. You've softened the balloon at that spot for a connecting joint.) Add to that a ½-inch (1.25-cm) ear-twist, another 2-inch (5-cm) bubble, another ½-inch (1.25-cm) ear-twist, and another 3-inch (7.5-cm) bubble. Guess what? You're halfway there!

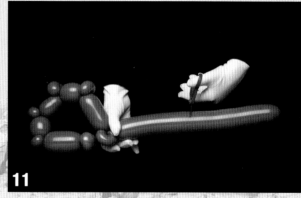

10

10) Make two ½-inch (1.25-cm) ear-twists.

11

11) Cut off any remaining balloon, tie it, and twist the stub around the last joint. You have a set of back legs.

12) Now retwist the middle ½-inch (1.25-cm) bubbles by twisting them at the joint between the tail and the body.

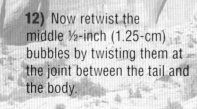

12

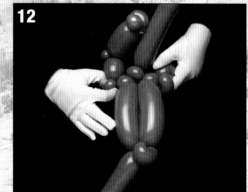

13) Untwist the ½-inch (1.25-cm) ear-twists at the knee joints to complete the legs.

14) Squeeze the tail a little to taper it.

15) Tie the tail end of a third balloon. Thread a 9-inch (23-cm) section of pipe cleaner into the balloon, and tie off the nozzle-end.

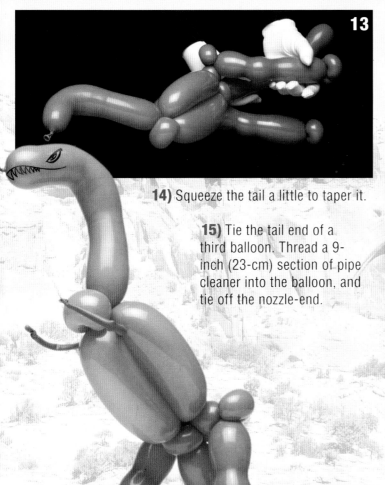

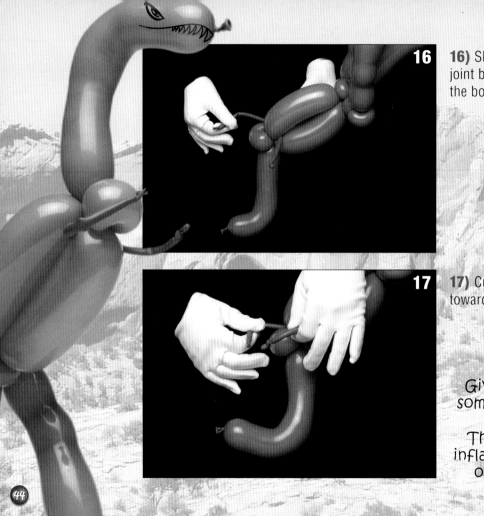

16) Slide the forelegs into the joint between the neck and the body.

17) Curve the claws in toward the body.

Give your dinosaur some facial features.

This raptor has an inflated opinion of its own viciousness!

TRICERAPOPS

Bigger than an elephant and twice the size of a rhinoceros,
the impressive plant-eating Triceratops could do some serious
damage to your grocery store's produce section!

1) Inflate two 260s, with 4-inch (10-cm) tails, then inflate two more about halfway.

2) Make three 3-inch (7.5-cm) bubbles (p. 6) on the nozzle-end of the first balloon, and lock-twist (p. 8) the second and third bubbles together.

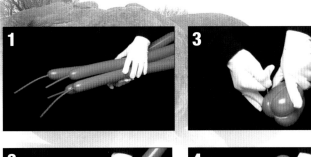

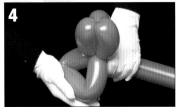

3) Grab the nozzle, pull it between the locked bubbles, and tuck it in.

4) Make an 8-inch (20-cm) loop-twist (p. 7) for the armored plate. Squeeze it a little to soften it, but don't break it. Your Triceratops will look tough, but it's a softie at heart!

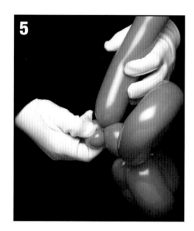

5) Make a 1 ½-inch (3.75-cm) bubble for the neck, and two ½-inch (1.25-cm) ear-twists (p. 11) after that.

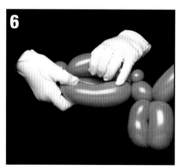

6) Make a three-bubble body with 6-inch (15-cm) bubbles, twisting the first two together and rolling the third one through the first two. Do you have a tailless, legless lump with a stump at the end? Perfect!

7) Now wrap the nozzle of the second balloon around the joint between the head and the neck.

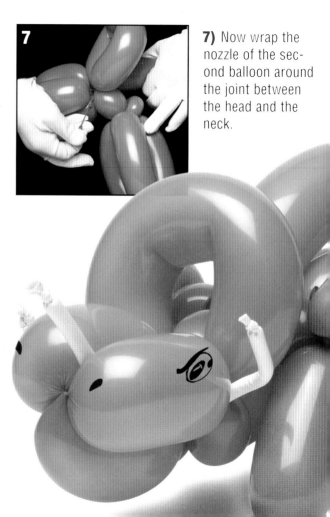

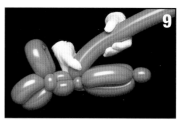

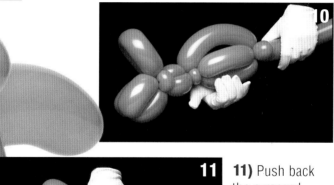

8) Make a 1 ½-inch (3.75-cm) bubble, and twist that around the joint between the neck and the body.

9) Make two ¾-inch (1.75-cm) ear-twists, positioning them on each side of the head.

10) Next, make an 8-inch (20-cm) bubble, and twist it around the last joint of the body, rolling it through the other three bubbles of the body.

11) Push back the armored plate (the loop-twist) so it sits on the 1 ½-inch (3.75-cm) neck bubble.

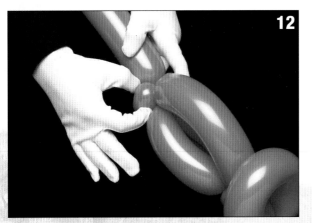

12) Let's lock that body in place. Tuck the original stump inside the body, and make two ear-twisted ½-inch (1.25-cm) bubbles at the back, repositioning as needed on either side.

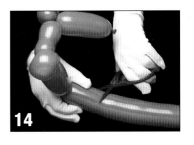

14) You're nearing the finish line! Using one of the remaining balloons, make a 4-inch (10-cm) bubble, a 1-inch (2.5-cm) ear-twisted bubble, two ½-inch (1.25-cm) bubbles, a 1-inch (2.5-cm) ear-twisted bubble, and a 4-inch (10-cm) bubble. Push the rest of the air down into the end of the balloon, pinch firmly, and cut off the excess uninflated balloon, tying it there. You have a set of legs.

The middle ½-inch (1.25-cm) bubbles came undone, and that's okay. You'll fix them in the next step.

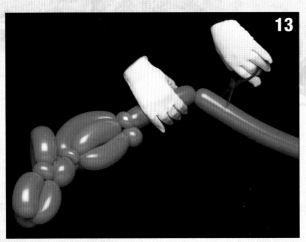

13) For the tail, make an 8-inch (20-cm) bubble. While holding the end of your bubble, cut off the remaining section of balloon. Tie it there, and curl (p. 9) your tail.

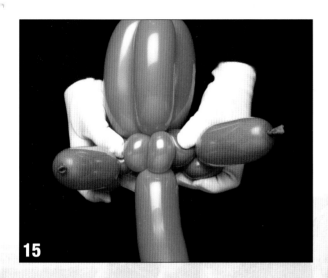

15

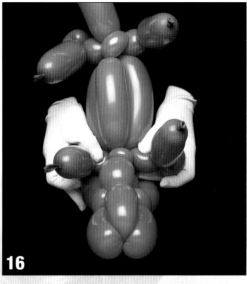

16

15) Retwist the middle ½-inch (1.25-cm) bubbles in the middle, and twist the legs onto the back of the body right in the center of the two ½-inch (1.25-cm) bubbles.

16) Repeat Steps 14-15 with the last balloon to make the next set of legs, twisting those onto the body between the neck and the head. Adjust the ½-inch (1.25-cm) bubbles to hold the legs in place.

17) Now you're ready for tusks. Cut a white 260 in half, and tie a knot just above the nozzle. Thread a pipe cleaner into that same half of balloon, and tie off the other end. Tie a knot in the tail-end of the other half of the balloon. Thread another pipe cleaner into that half, then tie off the other end.

18) Twist the longer section just below the armored plate, and tuck the shorter section between the front two face bubbles. Add a mouth and some eyes.

Tusk, tusk, tusk! It's been so much fun that it's almost a shame to be done!

NOT SO WOOLLY MAMMOTH

What, you don't have a barn big enough for a Woolly Mammoth? You'll love this pint-size prehistoric pet!

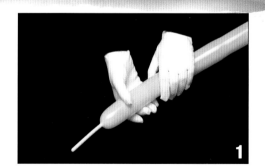

1) Inflate a 260, leaving a 4-inch (10-cm) tail.

2) Make a 3-inch (7.5-cm) tulip-twist (p. 9) on the nozzle- end.

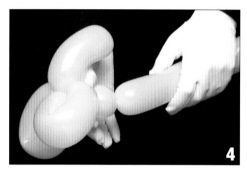

3) Make a 5-inch (12.5-cm) loop-twist (p. 7) for the first ear, and then lend it another ear with a second 5-inch (12.5-cm) loop twist.

4) Next, make a 1 ½-inch (3.75-cm) bubble (p. 6) for a neck.

5) For the front legs, make a 6-inch (15-cm) loop-twist.

6) At the tail of the balloon, make a 1-inch (2.5-cm) bubble, followed by another 6-inch (15-cm) loop-twist. Your mammoth now has back legs and a tail.

7) We're ready for tusks. Tie a knot in the tail-end of a white 260, and carefully thread a pipe cleaner into the balloon. Tie the nozzle-end.

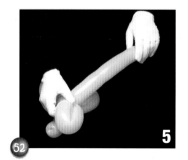

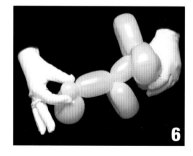

8) Feed the white balloon around the trunk, wrapping it around the joint. Bend the tusks upward into position and trim off the end of the nozzle at the knot. Don't forget the googly eyes!

You've brought this prehistoric giant down to size!

CATCH A TIGER BY THE TUSK

Earn your stripes by taming this Saber-Toothed Tiger!

1) Inflate two 260s, leaving 4-inch (10-cm) tails.

2) Now work on the upper jaw and snout. Make two 1 ½-inch (3.75-cm) bubbles (p. 6) on the nozzle-end, followed by a ½-inch (1.25-cm) bubble, and another 1 ½-inch (3.75-cm) bubble. Twist together the second and fourth bubbles in the series, and then ear-twist the ½-inch (1.25-cm) bubble. All the better to *smell* you with, my dear!

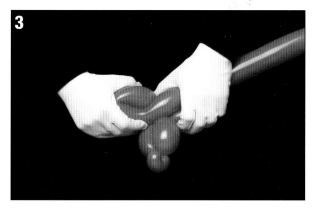

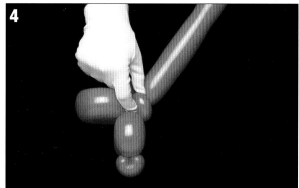

3) To give your tiger its characteristic mighty jaw, make a 4-inch (10-cm) loop-twist (p. 7).

4) Make two ½-inch (1.25-cm) ear-twisted bubbles (p. 11) for ears. Position them on either side of the head so your tiger can hear you coming from any direction.

5) To complete the head, wrap the nozzle around and through the upper jaw. Your tiger is putting its best face forward!

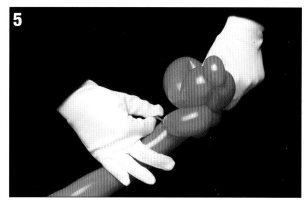

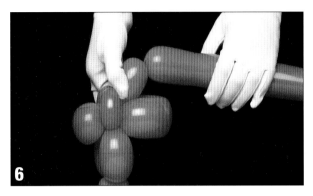

6) For the neck, make a 1 ½-inch (3.75-cm) bubble.

7) For front legs, make two 3 ½-inch (8.75-cm) bubbles, and lock-twist them (p. 8).

8) Using the second balloon, wrap the nozzle around the area just behind the head of your tiger, and make a 1 ½-inch (3.75-cm) bubble that will twist around the neck bubble to hold the head in place.

9) Holding the remaining sections of both balloons together. squeeze and twist together 6-inch (15-cm) bubbles to form part of the body.

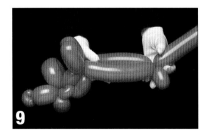

10

10) Make two ½-inch (1.25-cm) ear-twists to hold the body in place.

11) You're ready for back legs. Make two 3 ½-inch (8.75-cm) bubbles. and lock-twist them together.

12) Pull the remaining section of the second balloon back toward the body. and make a 6-inch (15-cm) bubble. rolling it through the other same-sized body bubbles.

13) Make another 6-inch (15-cm) bubble going back toward the tail, and wrap that joint around the tail joint a couple of times. Tuck the remaining stub of the first balloon inside the body.

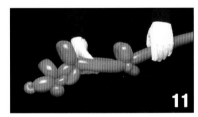

11

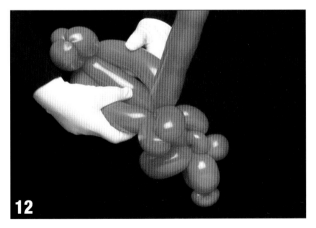

12

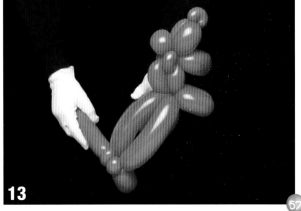

13

14) How can a predator be a predator if it can't see? To give your tiger eyes, tie a knot about 2-inches (5-cm) from the nozzle of a white balloon, and make a bubble there. Tie the end, and cut off the excess with scissors.

15) Divide that bubble in half, and slide them into place from below the mouth. To create smooth eyeballs (because no one likes bumpy ones), wrap the tie-ends around that joint. All the better to *see* you with, my dear!

16) A saber-toothed tiger isn't complete without tusks. Insert a 4-inch (10-cm) section of pipe cleaner into a white balloon. Cut off the remaining balloon, and tie off the nozzle-end.

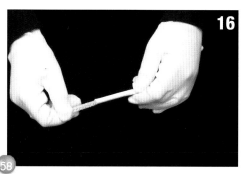

17

17) Slide the tusks down into the snout joint, and curve as needed. Be sure to give your tiger some eyes!

Feast your eyes on this wild cat!

JUST CALL HIM DON

The plant-eating Iguanadon found its feasts at the tops of trees.

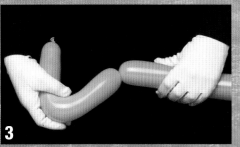

1) Inflate two 260s, leaving 4-inch (10-cm) tails on each.

2) Bend and pinch a 3-inch (7.5-cm) section of the nozzle-end of the first balloon to create a head.

3) To make the neck, form a 4-inch (10-cm) bubble (p. 6) below the bend

4) Just below that. make two 6-inch (15-cm) bubbles. and twist them together at the joint. Follow that with a ½-inch (1.25-cm) ear-twist (p. 11) to lock the body in place.

5) Make a series of bubbles: one 2-inch (5-cm) bubble. three ½-inch (1.25-cm) bubbles. and another 2-inch (5-cm) bubble for the legs. Twist together the first and fifth bubbles of that series. and position them facing out from the body.

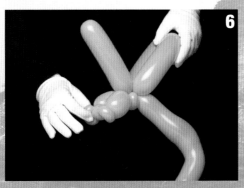

6) Ear-twist bubbles 2 and 4 (the outer ½-inch, or 1.25-cm. bubbles) of the long strand you just made. Twist each bubble four or five times to prevent the legs from deflating once you separate them.

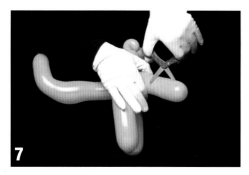

7) Using scissors, cut the end of the remaining bubble (remember to pinch it), and tie the knot. Wrap the loose end around the joint between the legs and neck, and tuck it in.

8) At the nozzle- end of the second balloon, make an 8-inch (20-cm) bubble. Slide it through the back of the body, and twist to lock in place.

9) Make another 6-inch (15-cm) bubble and twist it at the leg and neck joint for a third bubble on the body.

10) Bring the balloon back the other way, and make one more 6-inch (15-cm) bubble and twist together to complete the four-bubble body.

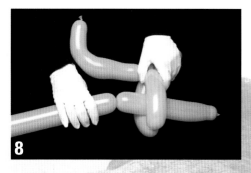

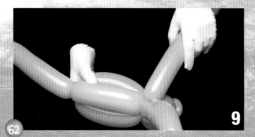

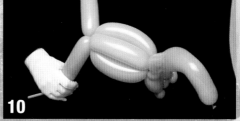

11) On the remaining end of the second balloon, repeat Steps 5-7 (pp. 61-62) for a five-bubble series that will form the back legs. Lock that around the joint between the tail and the body.

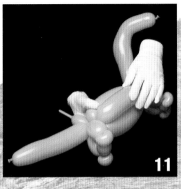

12) Using scissors, cut the middle bubble in each set of legs to separate them.

13) Pinch together any leftover section of balloon, cut it off, and tie it, wrapping the loose ends around the back leg joint. Then give your dinosaur a face!

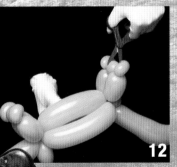

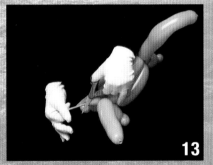

Keep houseplants out of the reach of this dinosaur!

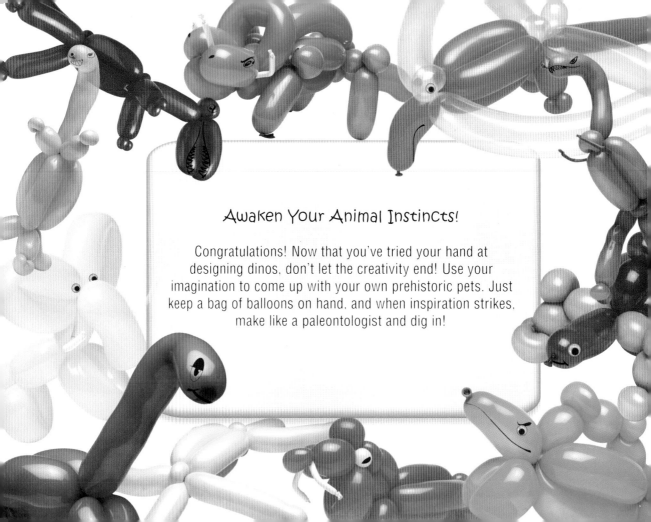

Awaken Your Animal Instincts!

Congratulations! Now that you've tried your hand at designing dinos, don't let the creativity end! Use your imagination to come up with your own prehistoric pets. Just keep a bag of balloons on hand, and when inspiration strikes, make like a paleontologist and dig in!